ROALD DAHL

WORDS OF
MAGICAL
MISCHIEF

Original text by
Roald Dahl

Illustrated by
Quentin Blake

Compiled by
Susan Rennie

IMPORTANT— READ THIS FIRST

This book contains **MAGIC WORDS**, **POTIONS** and **PARAPHERNALIA** that may cause tortoises to grow rapidly, or turn grandmas into beanpoles. (And if you don't know what *paraphernalia* means, you will if you keep reading.)

This is not a **SPELLBOOK**, but it does tell you about magic spells. Nor is it a **SPELLING BOOK**, but it will tell you how to spell and say some magic words — sometimes backwards.

Most Important of all, this book is **FOR CHIDDLERS**. If you suspect an adult of being a witch, **DO NOT LET THEM READ THIS BOOK!** It may give them ideas for how to hide their witchery — or worse, how to stop your own magic working.

So say OZIMUS ZOZIMUS, thrice time four...
Then turn the page for words galore!

— Susan Rennie

CONTENTS

MAKING Magical Mischief

'Some of us,' she said, 'have magic powers that can twist the creatures of this earth into wondrous shapes.'

— GEORGE'S MARVELLOUS MEDICINE

Many **magical** things happen in Roald Dahl's stories and poems, and there are **wondrous** words to describe every one of them — from **ARBADACARBA** to **ZOZIMUS!**

MAGIC MORSEL

The word **magic** comes from an ancient Persian word **magus**, meaning a priest.

MAGIC CAN:

make things (including grandmas) **disappear** or become **invisible** or **vanish into thin air.**

'And where's Georgina, my old mother? She's vanished!
... I saw her getting smaller and smaller and in the end
she got so small she just disappeared into thin air!'
— CHARLIE AND THE GREAT GLASS ELEVATOR

You can also say that someone has been **magicked away.**

make things (also including grandmas) GROW to become **GIGANTUOUS**, or **turn a peculiar colour.**

She was swelling! She was puffing up all over! Someone
was pumping her up, that's how it looked! Was she going to
explode! Her face was turning from purple to green!
— GEORGE'S MARVELLOUS MEDICINE

7

transform a **HUMAN BEAN** into a **NON-HUMAN BEAN** —for example, a boy into a mouse or a grown-up into a duck. You can also say that they have **metamorphosed**.

'The plain fact is,' my grandmother said,
'that your son Bruno has been rather drastically altered.'
'Altered!' shouted Mr Jenkins. 'What the devil d'you
mean altered?'
— THE WITCHES

'Oh! Oh! Oh! Oh!' sobbed Mrs Gregg. 'This is witches' work!' cried Mr Gregg. And both of them started running around the room, flapping their wings.
— THE MAGIC FINGER

Magic powers are also called

supernatural powers,

which means literally 'above nature'. (Although some magic works under the ground, like James's magic crystals.)

But what was it that the old man had said? Whoever they meet first, be it bug, insect, animal, or tree, that will be the one who gets the full power of their magic!
— JAMES AND THE GIANT PEACH

SAY THE magic word!

Magic words are **propsposterously** powerful—IF you say them correctly.

Mr Hoppy writes and says magic words *backwards*—so they become **cigam sdrow**. If you say them *exactly right*, they can make a tortoise grow **zippfizzingly** fast (but it will still move very slowly).

'My my, Alfie, you do seem hungry today,' *Mrs Silver was saying.* *'It must be Mr Hoppy's* *magic words I've been whispering to you.'*
— ESIO TROT

Here are some other **magic words** that you may find useful for working some magic of your own.

10

ABRACADABRA!

This famous magic word first appeared in an ancient Roman book of medicine as a charm to cure disease. If you say **Abracadabra** *backwards* like Mr Hoppy — and even better, *while also walking backwards* — it will very probably make the magic stronger (or at least more fun to perform):

Arbadacarba!

Hey PRESTO!

Some magicians like to say **Presto!** or **Hey Presto!** when they perform magic — and so does **Willy Wonka** when he creates magical confections such as **Television Chocolate**.

'Every single one of those millions of tiny pieces is fitted back into its right place (just like a jigsaw puzzle), and presto! — the photograph appears on the screen . . .'

— CHARLIE AND THE CHOCOLATE FACTORY

The word **presto** comes from Italian and means 'very quick', or **as fast as a fizzlecrump** — which is exactly the speed at which Mike Teavee is **magicked** inside a television.

You could also use another word meaning 'very fast' — then add an **-O** to make it sound **MORE MAGICAL**, for example:

Hey Whizzo!
or
Zippfizzo!

HOCUS-POCUS!

The word **hocus-pocus** is made up of
two parts that rhyme. Roald Dahl loved to
make words this way, like **flavory-savory**
and **Oompa Loompa**, and it is also a
duper super way to make
magic words. For example,
try saying

Ozimus Zozimus!

in a powerful voice . . .
and see what happens.

Hocus-pocus backwards is **SUCOP-SUCOH!** which is doubly magic — but sadly no longer rhymes.

A word or phrase that is the same backwards or forwards, like **dad** or **madam**, is called a **palindrome**. Note that it is tricky to spot a MAGIC palindrome, as it will look the same backwards and **forthwards**. So if Mr Hoppy were to shout

STEP ON NO PETS!

no one would know if those were magic words or not.

15

Open Sesame!

This magic phrase can open a wall
of solid rock, to reveal a secret cave.
It could therefore be useful for the
BFG if he ever forgets the entrance
to his cave.

The leader (it was surely he)
Now shouted, 'Open Sesame!'
And suddenly, surprise, surprise,
In front of Ali Baba's eyes,
The mighty rockface opened wide
To show a mammoth cave inside.

—RHYME STEW

Wordy Wizardry

Can you **concoct** a NEW **magic word**
made up of two parts that rhyme?
For example,

FRAZZLE-SWAZZLE!

WIZZLE-SWIZZLE!

or

OZERY-ZOZERY!

Splendiferous SPELLS

When you perform **MAGIC** on someone, you

bewitch or **enchant** them
or
cast a spell on them.

After that, they will be

bewitched or **enchanted** **spellbound** or **under a spell**.

The Grand High Witch plans to put every child in Inkland under her spell!

18

Note that if someone says they are **ENCHANTED**, it can *also* mean they are simply happy to see you (unless you have actually put them under a spell).

'Delighted to meet you, sir! Overjoyed! Enraptured! Enchanted!'

— CHARLIE AND THE CHOCOLATE FACTORY

Other words for a **magic spell** are **CHARM** and **INCANTATION**.

An evil spell is a **CURSE** or **HEX**. (Note that this is NOT the same as the type of cursing that Farmer Bunce does, which is very rude but not magic.)

To reverse a magic spell is to **undo** or **break** it. You could also try to **unmagic** it.

Note that it is NOT enough to say a charm *backwards* in order to break it. In fact, it might even make it DOUBLY magic. Saying a spell backwards is also the ONLY way to make it work on tortoises.

'The other words are spelled backwards, too,' Mr Hoppy said. 'If you turn them round into human language, they simply say: TORTOISE, TORTOISE, GET BIGGER BIGGER!'
— ESIO TROT

WITCHY WARNING!
Remember to add a **K** when you write the words **magicked** and **unmagicked**.

A book of spells is called a **spellbook**. Note that this is Very Different to a **spelling book**, which will tell you how to spell the word *newt*, but not how to turn Miss Trunchbull into one. *It is very important not to confuse the two types of book.*

Potent POTIONS

'Here we go, then!' cried George, jumping up from the table. 'A magic medicine it shall be!'
— GEORGE'S MARVELLOUS MEDICINE

It is essential to use the right ingredients when making a **magic potion** — or it could be a **catasterous disastrophe!** But you must also use the right words for the instructions.

STAGE 1

Invent a magic recipe, **formulate** a magic **formula** or **concoct** a magic **concoction**.

'Next', continued The Grand High Witch, 'you vill prepare yourselves for this Great Gala Opening by filling every choc and every sveet in your shop with my very latest and grrreatest magic formula!'
— THE WITCHES

22

STAGE 2

Assemble the magic **INGREDIENTS**. (If they are Very Rare, like gruntles' eggs, you may have to **hunt**, **forage** or **track** them down.)

Some ideas are:

telescopes
or **telescoops**
(for boiling)

alarm clocks
(for roasting)

mouse-tails
(for frying)

squerkles
(of the venomous variety)

Best FROG JUICE

frog juice
(best quality only)

23

gruntles' eggs
(yolks only)

giant curlicues
(the curlier the better)

perfume of **turnip flowers**
(for **ROTSOME** aroma)

slimy squigglers
(fresh from the sea)

'Next', said The Grand High Witch,
'you take your boiled telescope and
your frrried mouse-tails and your
cooked mice and your rrroasted
alarm-clock and all together you
put them into the mixer.'
— THE WITCHES

24

STAGE 3

Add each ingredient to a **GIGANTUOUS** saucepan or
(if you are lucky enough to have one) a colossal **cauldron**.
You might need to **stir** or **swizzle** the mixture vigorously.

A **sizzlepan**, which the BFG uses to fry
snozzcumbers, is too shallow to brew a whole
magic potion. Another option is the **skull of a
dead witch**, but those are trickier to find than
gruntles' eggs.

*'Crocodile tongues!' he cried. 'One
thousand long slimy crocodile tongues
boiled up in the skull of a dead witch
for twenty days and nights with the
eyeballs of a lizard!'*
— JAMES AND THE GIANT PEACH

MAGIC MORSEL

The word **cauldron**
comes from a Latin
word **calidus**, meaning
'hot'.

A **snipsy** amount of a magic ingredient is

a **drop** or **dash** or **splash** or a **pinch** or **sprinkle**.

Mr Wonka opened the bottle and dripped four drops of oily black liquid into Charlie's spoon.

— CHARLIE AND THE GREAT GLASS ELEVATOR

A generous amount of liquid is a **slosh**. For extra strength or **potency**, be like George and tip in a whole **bottleful**.

WITCHY WARNING!
Note that the plural of **bottleful** is **bottlefuls**: *The recipe calls for two bottlefuls of frog juice.*

26

STAGE 4

Let the magic mixture **brew** and **stew**. It might

boil or **seethe** or **smoke** or **simmer**
fizz or **sizzle** or **froth** or **foam**.

Magical **fumes** or **vapours** might

curl or **swirl** or **whirl** upwards, or **whiffle** or **swishwiffle** through the air.

*Soon the marvellous mixture
began to froth and foam. A rich
blue smoke, the colour of peacocks,
rose from the surface of the liquid,
and a fiery fearsome smell filled
the kitchen.*

— GEORGE'S MARVELLOUS
MEDICINE

27

To strengthen the magic, chant a **brewing charm**, like George:

And suddenly, George found himself dancing
around the steaming pot, chanting strange
words that came into his head out of nowhere:
 'Fiery broth and witch's brew
Foamy froth and riches blue
Fume and spume and spoondrift spray
 Fizzle swizzle shout hooray.'
— GEORGE'S MARVELLOUS MEDICINE

ONOMATOPOEIC (say on-o-mat-o-**pee**-ik) words, which sound like the thing they describe, are especially good for chanting. Try using any (and preferably ALL) of the following:

bubble, bibble,
fuzzle, fizzle, hiss, hizzle,
squizzle, swizzle.

Note that for the charm to **take effect**, you must chant (and dance) **with gusto!**

MAGIC MORSEL

In William Shakespeare's play *Macbeth*, the three witches also chant a brewing charm:

Double double toil and trouble, fire burn and caldron bubble.

STAGE 5

Bottle the mixture in a special jar, like the BFG's precious dream jars. A small glass flask for keeping magical potions is called a **phial** (say **fy**-ull).

Label it with a helpful name that tells you what the magic does, like **DELAYED ACTION MOUSE-MAKER** or **INSTANT ACTION FROG-MAKER** or **DOUBLE STRENGTH DREADED SHRINKS FORMULA**.

A **portion** of magic potion is called a **dose**.

'Mother!' wailed Mrs Kranky. 'You've just drunk fifty doses of George's Marvellous Medicine Number Four and look what one tiny spoonful did to that little old brown hen!'

— GEORGE'S MARVELLOUS MEDICINE

POWERFUL Paraphernalia

Paraphernalia (say para-fer-**nail**-ee-a) means 'equipment or general bits and bobs that you carry around with you'.

Here are some items of magical **paraphernalia** used by magicians of all sorts.

⭐ MAGIC BEANS or CRYSTALS

Magic beans and crystals work their magic *slo-o-o-owly*, sometimes overnight. They can make an ordinary peach tree or bean plant into a magical and magnificent one.

31

You might **strew** or **scatter** magic beans on the ground, or plant or bury them under-ground.

'There's more power and magic in those things in there than in all the rest of the world put together,' the old man said softly.
— JAMES AND THE GIANT PEACH

MAGIC LAMP

To make a magic lamp work you must rub or polish it. If you do this in exactly the right way, a **genie** (say **jean**-ee) or **djinn** (say jin) will appear and grant you a wish (or three).

And suddenly in clouds of smoke
Appeared the most amazing bloke,
A sort of genie or a djinn,
An ugly brute with scarlet skin
And purple tassels in his hair
And nothing on but underwear.
— RHYME STEW

33

MAGIC MIRROR

A magic mirror will tell you the answer to **biffsquiggling** or brain-boggling questions.

If you ask a magic mirror about the future (for example, to ask what Willy Wonka will do next), it is called **scryomancy** (say **skry-o-man-see**).

This was a mirror framed in brass,
A MAGIC TALKING LOOKING-GLASS.
Ask it something day or night,
It always got the answer right.
— REVOLTING RHYMES

MAGIC WAND

You might **flick**, **swish** or **swoosh** a magic wand, or **zap** someone with its power.

An old word for a magic wand is a **charming rod**.

The Fairy said ,'Hang on a tick'.
She gave her wand a mighty flick
And quickly, in no time at all,
Cindy was at the Palace Ball!
— REVOLTING RHYMES

34

Wordy Wizardry

You can add the ending **-MANCY** to invent a new type of fortune-telling. For example, studying cloud shapes could be **CLOUDOMANCY**.

Of course if you see some Cloud-Men, you can safely predict that there will be bad weather very soon!

MAGICAL Body Parts

 ## MAGIC FINGER

Magical fingers look just like un-magical fingers — until you get angry and then they start to **spark** and **flash**.

A sort of flash comes out of me, a quick flash, like something electric. It jumps out and touches the person who has made me cross . . . And after that . . . things begin to happen.
— THE MAGIC FINGER

MAGICAL NECK

Magical necks (which can *stre-e-e-tch*) are Very Rare, but they are extraordinarily useful for window-cleaning.

'Your Grace', the Giraffe said, giving the Duke a small superior smile, 'there are no windows in the world I cannot reach with this magical neck of mine.'
— THE GIRAFFE AND THE PELLY AND ME

MAGICAL NOSE

The Red-Hot Smoke-Belching Gruncher has a magical nose that can sniff a Minpin or **human bean** from ten miles away.

The fearsome Gruncher . . . has grunched up hundreds of humans and literally millions of Minpins. What makes him so dangerous is his amazing and magical nose.
— THE MINPINS

WITCHY words for Witch-Spotters

Witches have been around for so long that **human beans** have come up with dillions of words to describe them and their **WITCHY** magic.

The magic that witches do is called

witchcraft or witchery or wizardry or sorcery

'Didn't I tell you I had magic powers! Didn't I warn you I had wizardry in the tips of my fingers!'
— GEORGE'S MARVELLOUS MEDICINE

'If we brought this off, it would be the greatest triumph in the whole history of witchery!'
— THE WITCHES

Note that **sorcery** has NOTHING to do with saucers. A **Quogwinkle** might travel through space in a *flying saucer* — but a *flying sorcerer* is something very different!

Something that reminds you of a witch (like a **rotsome** smell or a grumpy grandma) is **witch-like** or **witchy**.

Oh, how he hated Grandma!
He really hated that horrid old
witchy woman.
— GEORGE'S MARVELLOUS
MEDICINE

A good way to test if someone is a witch is to ask them to **unglove** or remove their gloves.

If you are Very Brave, you could also try to **unmask** or **unwig** a witch. If a group or roomful of witches were to **unwig** all at once, you would see a sea of scratchy scalps.

There now appeared in front of me row upon row of bald female heads, a sea of naked scalps, every one of them red and itchy-looking.
— THE WITCHES

Wordy Wizardry

You can **concoct** new synonyms for the word **witchy** by changing the ending. For example, **WITCHFUL**, **WITCHSOME** — or even **WITCHICIOUS** (to rhyme with *vicious*).

WHAT DO YOU CALL A witch?

It is a VERY BAD idea to be impolite to a witch.
You must never call a witch a **grizzly old grunion**.
But it is USUALLY safe to call them a

Sorcerer or Sorceress.

There are no male witches in Roald
Dahl's stories, but if you were to meet
one elsewhere, you would call them a

wizard or warlock.

The word **wizard** is more than 500 years old (as old
as some wizards) and originally meant 'a wise man'.
But **witch** is EVEN OLDER and was first used in
English over 1000 years ago.

Some people call witches **hags**, but it is UNWISE to call a real witch that (or a grandma that you suspect of being a witch).

Little George stood by the door staring at the old hag
in the chair. She stared back at him. Could it be,
George wondered, that she was a witch?
— GEORGE'S MARVELLOUS MEDICINE

When addressing the Grand High Witch, it is best to use a splendid title such as

Your Grand Highness or
Your Splendiferousness

and most definitely NOT

Your Ugliness or **Your Wizenedness**
or **Your Rotsomeness**.

43

However, even if you call a witch by a POLITE name, she might

FRY you to a FRAZZLE

or

SWIZZLE you to a SWAZZLE

anyway—just for FUN.

A group or gathering of witches is called a **coven**—which rhymes with *oven*. This makes it a Useful Word for poems or recipes that involve roasting alarm-clocks and other magic ingredients:

A sorceress and her witchy coven
Were roasting alarm-clocks in an oven.

A **human bean** who seems to have magic powers, like Willy Wonka, is a **MAGICIAN**.

Someone who only *pretends* to have magic powers, by performing magic tricks, is a **CONJUROR**.

MAGIC MORSEL

An old word for a wizard or magician was **wonder-master**, which perfectly describes Willy Wonka!

'Clever!' cried the old man. 'He's more than that! He's a magician with chocolate! He can make anything — anything he wants!'

— CHARLIE AND THE CHOCOLATE FACTORY

45

MAGICAL CREATURES

A **FAMILIAR** is an animal, such as a cat or a bat, that is kept by a witch because of its **magic powers**.

A **GRIMALKIN** (say gri-**mal**-kin) is a very old witch's cat. Grimalkins are usually female, and some are as old as witches (which is **jumpsquifflingly** old). Willy Wonka adds the teeth of an ancient Mexican grimalkin to his magical ageing potion, **Vita-Wonk**.

The **GRUNTLE** is a bird that nests high up in tall trees in order to avoid predators — especially **witches** who steal its eggs for their potions.

'Vhile the mixer is still mixing you must add to it the yolk of vun grrruntle's egg.' 'A gruntle's egg!' cried the audience. 'We shall do that!'
— THE WITCHES

46

These Very Rare creatures have **extra-usual** body parts which are much prized by witches for their **magical properties**.

The **BLABBERSNITCH** is a sea-creature with a **swashboggling** beak.

The **CATSPRINGER** is a burrowing creature with an **extra-usual** tongue.

The **CRABCRUNCHER** has **propsposterously** powerful claws.

The **GROBBLESQUIRT** has a **splendiferous** snout.

'So you mix in the egg,' The Grand High Witch went on, 'and vun after the other you also mix in the following items: the claw of a crrrabcrrruncher, the beak of a blabbersnitch, the snout of a grrrobblesqvirt and the tongue of a catsprrringer.'

— THE WITCHES

ZOZIMUSSY Mixtures

> 'Dreams is not like human beans or animals. They has no brains. They is made of zozimus.'
> — THE BFG

The dreams in Dream Country are made from a mysterious and magical substance called **zozimus**.

If you see something as magically mysterious as **zozimus**, you could describe it as

zozimussy.

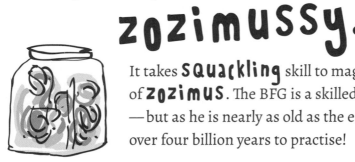

It takes **squackling** skill to magic dreams out of **zozimus**. The BFG is a skilled dream **magician** —but as he is nearly as old as the earth, he has had over four billion years to practise!

PHANTASMAGORIA

(say fan-taz-ma-**go**-ree-a)

The word **phantasmagoria** means a series of dream-like **wispy-misty** shapes or images — just the sort of things you might see **whiffling** through the air in Dream Country.

'Dreams,' he said, 'is very mysterious things. They is floating around in the air like little wispy-misty bubbles.'
— THE BFG

Human beans have only one word for a bad dream —

A NIGHTMARE.

But in Dream Country, there are SIX different names for dreams, depending on whether they are good or **ghastly**.

'I is catching a frightsome troggglehumper!' he cried. 'This is a bad bad dream! It is worse than a bad dream! It is a nightmare!'
— THE BFG

Ghastly dreams are called

bogthumpers
and
grobswitchers
and the very worst, ghastliest dreams are

trogglehumpers.

MAGIC MORSEL
The word **nightmare** comes from an old word **mare**, which meant an evil spirit that caused bad dreams.

50

Good dreams are called

ringbellers
and
winksquifflers

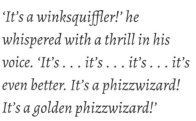

but the best, most splendiferous dreams are

golden phizzwizards.

'It's a winksquiffler!' he whispered with a thrill in his voice. 'It's . . . it's . . . it's . . . it's even better. It's a phizzwizard! It's a golden phizzwizard!'

— THE BFG

51

MAGIC MORSEL
The **baku** is a magical creature from Japan. It will eat your bad dreams if you ask for its help.

Grobswitchy dreams have some nasty sounding names in other languages too.

A **TROGGLEHUMPER** is called:

trollenklopper in Dutch

troglopompe in French

troglogobo in Italian

trauchlefasher in Scots

jorobanoches (say ho-ro-bah-**no**-chez) in Spanish, meaning 'night nuisance'

52

Wordy Wizardry

Try making a new word by respelling words like *fantastic* or *fantabulous* with **PH-** to make **PHANTASTIC** and **PHANTABULOUS**.

They will instantly look more magical and **PHIZZ-WHIZZING!**

The WITCHING HOUR

The BFG pours dreams into sleeping **chiddlers** at the most magical time of night — the **witching hour**. Willy Wonka calls it the **witchy hour of gloomness**.

MAGIC MORSEL

William Shakespeare also wrote about the **witching hour**. A ghostly scene in his play *Hamlet* takes place during the witching time of night.

The witching hour . . . was a special moment in the middle of the night when every child and every grown-up was in a deep deep sleep, and all the dark things came out from hiding and had the world to themselves.

— THE BFG

In the **witching hour**, frightswiping
creatures may **EMERGE** and start to:

creep or crawl
gliss or hiss
prowl or roam
scurry or scutter

slither,
slime,
or
ooze

At the witchy hour of gloomness,
All the grobes come oozing home.
You can hear them softly slimeing,
Glissing hissing o'er the slubber,
All those oily boily bodies
Oozing onward in the gloam.

— CHARLIE & THE GREAT
GLASS ELEVATOR

GHASTLY Ghosts

'I know it's a ghost!' Matilda said. 'I've heard it here before! This room is haunted! I thought you knew that.'

— MATILDA

Ghosts come in many shapes and sizes — and also many words, including: **APPARITION SPIRIT SPECTRE PHANTOM.**

A **HAUNTED** (say **hont**-id) place is one where ghosts **linger** or **lurk**, especially in the **witching hour**.

Something that looks or sounds like a **wispy-misty ghost** is **ghostly** or **spectral**.

The ghostly shadow of Grandma Georgina's face was no more than a yard away now.

— CHARLIE AND THE GREAT GLASS ELEVATOR

Something as **frightsome** as a **ghost** is

CREEPY or SPOOKY or EERIE or UNCANNY.

'Rattle my bones!' the parrot said, giving a wonderful imitation of a spooky voice. 'Rattle my bones!'

— MATILDA

Gradually it grew darker and darker, and then a pale three-quarter moon came up over the tops of the clouds and cast an eerie light over the whole scene.

— JAMES AND THE GIANT PEACH

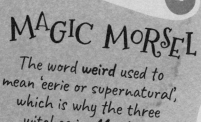

MAGIC MORSEL

The word **weird** used to mean 'eerie or supernatural', which is why the three witches in *Macbeth* are called the *Weird Sisters*— not because they are a bit odd!

A **GHOUL** is a type of evil spirit, and something **ghoulish** (say **gool**-ish) is wicked and cruel, like an evil ghoul.

The witches gasped. They gaped. They turned and gave each other ghoulish grins of excitement.
— THE WITCHES

If you are **AGHAST** (say a-**gast**), you are horrified by something. For example, Sophie is **aghast** at the thought of a **murderful** giant eating the Queen.

'The Fleshlumpeater is longing dearly to guzzle her up', the BFG said, smiling a little now. 'Who, the Queen?' Sophie cried, aghast.
— THE BFG

WITCHY WARNING!

Remember the silent letter **H** in the words **ghost**, **aghast** and **ghastly**. Think of the **H** in the word **haunt** to help you remember!

58

The word **GHASTLY** is related to **ghost** and used to mean 'terrifying', but now it usually means '**horrigust** or nasty', like Aunts Sponge and Spiker.

And there they sat, these two ghastly hags, sipping their drinks, and every now and again screaming at James to chop faster and faster.
— JAMES AND THE GIANT PEACH

MYSTERIOUS SuperPowers

Some **human beans**, like Matilda, have powers which can seem magical — and are definitely **extra-usual!**

Superpowers are also called **superhuman** (or **super-humanbean**) powers, or **paranormal** powers.

PSYCHOKINESIS (say sigh-ko-ki-**nees**-iss) or **TELEKINESIS** is the power that Matilda has to make an object move without touching it, just by focusing her mind.

'I can do it!' she cried. 'I can really do it! I can pick the cigar up just with my eye-power and push it and pull it in the air any way I want!'
— MATILDA

60

LEVITATION is when something rises and hovers or floats through the air as if by magic—for example, a piece of chalk starting to write on its own.

Nigel, at the other end of the room, jumped to his feet and started pointing excitedly at the blackboard and screaming, 'The chalk! The chalk! Look at the chalk! It's moving all on its own!'

— MATILDA

A **PHENOMENON** (say fe-**nom**-in-on) is something **extra-usual** that you can see but can't fully explain, like Matilda's **extra-usual** powers.

'I am trying to explain to you,' Miss Honey said patiently, 'that we are dealing with the unknown. It is an unexplainable thing. The right word for it is a phenomenon.'

— MATILDA

AND FINALLY...

Roald Dahl wrote about lots of other things, too — such as BEARDS, BLUEBERRIES, CARAVANS, CROCODILES, CHOCOLATE and CHIDDLERS.

You can find ALL of these and SQUILLIONS more in the *phizz-whizzing* **Oxford Roald Dahl Thesaurus** ...

... and of course in the splendiferous stories and poems of ROALD DAHL.

OXFORD

Oxford ROALD DAHL Thesaurus

All the words you need for magic, **marvels** and **mischief**